DISASTER ALERT!

HURRICANES

Harvey Irma Maria and Nate

Julia Sillett

CRABTREE
PUBLISHING COMPANY
WWW.CRABTREEBOOKS.COM

CRABTREE
PUBLISHING COMPANY
WWW.CRABTREEBOOKS.COM

Author: Julia Sillett

Project coordinator: Kathy Middleton

Editor: Ellen Rodger

Proofreader and Indexer: Wendy Scavuzzo

Design: Margaret Amy Salter

Photo research: Margaret Amy Salter

Production coordinator
and prepress technician: Margaret Amy Salter

Print coordinator: Katherine Berti

Cover: Hurricanes form from tropical waves over the Atlantic Ocean.

Title page: Realistic 3-D illustration of a hurricane approaching the USA. Elements of this image are provided by NASA.

Photographs:
Creative Commons: p 25 (bottom)
FEMA: p 26
Getty: Pool, p 27
National Guard: p 14
NOAA Photo Library: Lieut. Commander Mark Moran, p 39; Mike Mascaro p 19 (top right)
Shutterstock: JEAN-FRANCOIS Manuel, pp 4, 28, 45; michelmond, pp 11 (top right), 16; DFree, p13 (top right); All Stock Photos, p 15; Felix Mizioznikov, p 24 (bottom); Alessandro Pietri, p 31 (top); Rena Schild, p 32; Sara Armas, p 35; Pattie Steib, p 41 (inset); Lori Martin, p 42; AMFPhotography, p 44
U.S. Department of Defense: Lance Cpl. Niles Lee, p 12
Scott Air Force Base: Snow, p 17 (top left); Tech. Sgt. Zachary Wolf, p 17 (bottom); Ryan DeCamp, p 25 (top);
U.S. National Guard: Staff Sgt. Daniel J. Martinez, front cover
Wikimedia Commons: p 8; p 11 (bottom); p 13 (bottom); p 23 (inset); p 24 (top right); p 29; Puerto Rico National Guard, p 33 (bottom left); p 33 (bottom right), Andrea Booher / FEMA, p 34; p 38; The National Guard, pp 40, 41 (bottom);

All other images are from Shutterstock.

Library and Archives Canada Cataloguing in Publication

Sillett, Julia, author
    Hurricanes Harvey, Irma, Maria, and Nate / Julia Sillett.

(Disaster alert!)
Includes index.
Issued in print and electronic formats.
ISBN 978-0-7787-5175-5 (hardcover).--
ISBN 978-0-7787-5184-7 (softcover).--
ISBN 978-1-4271-2112-7 (HTML)

    1. Hurricanes--History--21st century--Juvenile literature. 2. Hurricanes-
-Juvenile literature. 3. Disaster relief--Juvenile literature. I. Title. II. Series:
Disaster alert!

HV635.5.S55 2018   j363.34'922   C2018-902966-8
                                                C2018-902967-6

Library of Congress Cataloging-in-Publication Data

Names: Sillett, Julia, author.
Title: Hurricanes Harvey, Irma, Maria, and Nate / Julia Sillett.
Description: New York, New York : Crabtree Publishing, 2019. | Series: Disaster alert! | Includes index.
Identifiers: LCCN 2018035792 (print) | LCCN 2018037672 (ebook) | ISBN 9781427121127 (Electronic) | ISBN 9780778751755 (hardcover) | ISBN 9780778751847 (pbk.)
Subjects: LCSH: Hurricanes--Juvenile literature.
Classification: LCC QC944.2 (ebook) | LCC QC944.2 .S54 2019 (print) | DDC 363.34/922--dc23
LC record available at https://lccn.loc.gov/2018035792

Crabtree Publishing Company
www.crabtreebooks.com   1-800-387-7650

Printed in the U.S.A./102018/CG20180907

Published in Canada
Crabtree Publishing
616 Welland Ave.
St. Catharines, ON
L2M 5V6

Published in the United States
Crabtree Publishing
PMB 59051
350 Fifth Avenue, 59th Floor
New York, New York

Published in the United Kingdom
Crabtree Publishing
Maritime House
Basin Road North, Hove

Published in Australia
Crabtree Publishing
3 Charles Street
Coburg North
VIC, 3058

Table of Contents

Pounding Storms

During 2017, four powerful hurricanes left paths of destruction along the Atlantic coast of North America, the Caribbean, and the Gulf of Mexico. These epic storms, hurricanes Harvey, Irma, Maria, and Nate, left hundreds of people dead and millions of lives forever altered.

A Season of Destruction

The Atlantic Hurricane season happens every year between June 1 and November 30. But 2017 was especially damaging because of warm waters in the Atlantic Ocean and dangerous weather patterns in the air above it. Hurricane Harvey was the first of the four to **wreak havoc**. It made landfall in Texas during late August.

In September, Hurricane Irma made its way from the Caribbean and tore through Florida. Shortly after, Hurricane Maria devastated Puerto Rico. In October, Hurricane Nate tore through Costa Rica, Nicaragua, Honduras, and finally Louisiana and Mississippi.

What's the Damage?

The total damages are still unclear, but experts say that for the United States alone, 2017 was the most expensive and active in the country's history, at over $250 billion.

Hurricane Season

The Caribbean Sea, and the Gulf of Mexico are particularly at risk for hurricanes that originate in the Atlantic Ocean. On average, 10 tropical storms develop in the Atlantic each year and grow into hurricanes. There were 17 different storms recorded in 2017, making it an abnormally active season. Hurricanes Harvey, Irma, Maria, and Nate were particularly strong storms, which added to the devastation. In fact, because of the records broken during this year, the **World Meteorological Organization (WMO)** has retired their names. There will never be other hurricanes with these names.

Hurricane Nate caused 48 deaths, 14 in Costa Rica alone. It was that country's costliest natural disaster.

Naming a Hurricane

Male and female names have been used to refer to storms since 1953. Storms used to be named using geographic *coordinates*, but they began using names because they were easier to communicate back and forth between scientists, meteorologists, and the media.

A Recipe for Disaster

A hurricane is a type of weather system known as a tropical cyclone. "Cyclone" is the general term used for all **circulating** weather systems.

A cyclone is called a hurricane when it develops over the Atlantic **Basin** and when the winds reach 74 mph (119 kph).

A hurricane starts when a low **air pressure** system forms over warm water. Low air pressure is created when the air above the water is warm and moist. The warm air rises, so there is less pressure in the center of the system.

This warm air moves upward in a counter-clockwise circular motion, into cooler parts of the **atmosphere**. The molecules in the air cool to become water molecules, which then form clouds.

The surrounding air with higher pressure fills in the space where the warm air is rising. This happens repeatedly, and creates "swirls" of wind in the air.

This continues happening and the system of air pressure, winds and cloud gains strength, rotating faster and faster.

Saffir-Simpson Hurricane Wind Scale

1 Wind speeds of 74 to 95 mph (120–153 kph). Category 1 storms damage homes, snap tree branches, and knock down power lines and poles.

2 Wind speeds of 96 to 110 mph (154–177 kph). Category 2 storms have extremely dangerous winds that can cause major roof damage, shallowly rooted trees can snap, and power outages can last days or weeks.

3 Wind speeds of 111 to 129 mph (179-208 kph). Category 3 storms cause devastating damage including snapped or uprooted trees blocking roads, and electricity and water can be unavailable for several days.

4 Wind speeds of 130 to 156 mph (209–251 kph). Category 4 storms cause catastrophic damage, including severe damage to homes, most trees snapped or uprooted, widespread power outages lasting weeks to months. Affected areas unlivable for weeks or months.

5 Wind speeds of 157 mph (253 kph) and up. Category 5 storms cause catastrophic damage with a high percentage of homes totally destroyed. Power outages can last from weeks to months and the affected areas won't be livable for weeks or months afterward.

The "eye" of the storm is at the center of the hurricane. It is a space usually around 20 to 40 miles (32–64 km) wide. It is the calmest area of the storm with clear skies and low air pressure.

Hurricane Harvey

Wind and Rain Unleashed

Hurricane Harvey was the first major hurricane to make landfall in the United States since 2005—a year marked by the devastating hurricanes Katrina and Wilma. Harvey moved through the Caribbean and the Yucatan Peninsula as a tropical storm before gaining strength and hurricane status. It would go on to make landfall three times over the course of six days, taking 88 lives and costing more than $125 billion in damage.

A Wave to a Hurricane

It all began with a **tropical wave** off the west coast of Africa on Sunday, August 13, 2017, which met with a low-pressure weather system. Harvey quickly turned from a **tropical depression** to a major hurricane over the course of only 40 hours. By Thursday, August 17, the National Hurricane Center issued warnings for Hurricane Harvey, and it hit the Windward Islands on Friday, August 18.

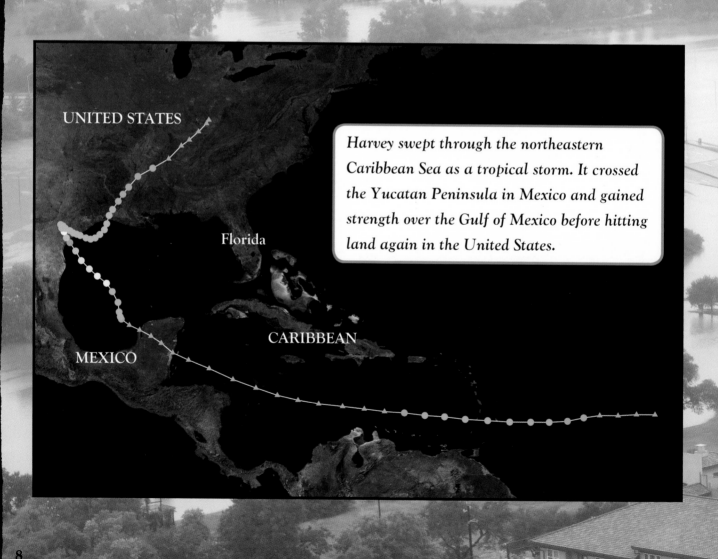

UNITED STATES

Florida

CARIBBEAN

MEXICO

Harvey swept through the northeastern Caribbean Sea as a tropical storm. It crossed the Yucatan Peninsula in Mexico and gained strength over the Gulf of Mexico before hitting land again in the United States.

Making Landfall

Harvey hit Texas on August 25, 2017 over northern San José Island. It was 280 miles (451 km) wide, and had winds of 130 miles per hour (209 kph) when it hit near Rockport. On August 26, Harvey was downgraded to a tropical storm. The damage continued with the rains and flooding afterward, affecting 13 million people in Texas, Louisiana, Mississippi, Tennessee, and Kentucky.

A Wave

The tail end of the storm met with warm water and underwent **rapid intensification**—a process in which winds increase by at least 35 miles per hour (56 kph) during a 24-hour period. Rapid intensification is difficult for meteorologists to predict because there are so many unknown factors. It also makes storms extra dangerous to people and places. After the storm was upgraded, extreme wind warnings were released. It wasn't long before the winds became so strong that they destroyed the measuring equipment before the speed could be recorded.

In Its Path

In Texas, Rockport and Fulton were hit directly by the storm and suffered the most damage. Buildings were destroyed, there were power outages, and residents lost access to water. Even 30 miles (48 km) away in Corpus Christi, strong and damaging wind gusts were experienced. Before the storm was downgraded, there was also significant damage to the coastal towns of Port Lavaca, Copano Village, Aransas Pass, Port Aransas, and Ingleside.

A Costly Disaster

Hurricane Harvey was the second most expensive natural disaster in U.S. history, second only to Hurricane Katrina in 2005.

Wind and Rain

The hurricane touching down was only the start of the devastation in Texas. The rain that followed the hurricane created new problems for Texans when an estimated 33 trillion gallons (125 trillion liters) of water flooded the area between Houston and southwest Louisiana.

The Rain Remains

The rain continued from Saturday, August 26, until Tuesday, August 29. Hurricanes create rain when they pass over warm ocean waters, drawing water vapor into the atmosphere. The vapor cools and eventually turns into **precipitation**. The U.S. record for rainfall in a single storm was broken after a total rainfall of 60.58 inches (153.87 cm) of rain was measured in Port Arthur. The National Weather Service had to add new colors to its maps in order to show total rainfalls that were higher than 30 inches (76.2 cm)—a new record.

Although the winds were intense, Harvey was a **slow-moving storm** system, which meant it stayed over Texas for days, even after it was downgraded to a tropical storm. Often, there will be another weather system high in the atmosphere around the area of the hurricane that will force the storm in a different direction. In the case of Harvey, there was no weather system or high winds in the upper atmosphere to disturb the hurricane's weather system. The longer a hurricane stays over one place, the more rain it drops in one place.

Floodwaters

With record-breaking rainfall came severe flooding. Concrete-covered cities such as Houston were no match for the amount of rain that fell. The flooding was made worse because much of Houston is flat and there is so much pavement covering the ground from **suburb** developments. Pavement and concrete do not absorb water like soil, so the rain couldn't be absorbed into the ground as it naturally would. The city's **reservoirs** also could not handle so much rain in such a short period of time. Floodwaters were released from **dams**, which made houses and buildings vulnerable to flooding.

Two men wade through water after Harvey flooded their Houston neighborhood.

Mattress Mack to the Rescue

During the floods of Hurricane Harvey, one man decided to do what he could to help those in need. Jim McIngvale, popularly known as Mattress Mack, opened two of his Gallery Furniture stores to provide food and shelter to hundreds of people stranded by the storm. His stores are built on concrete higher above the ground to be safe from floods. The stores provided a safe place for people to seek shelter.

Rescue Missions

As the floodwaters flowed through streets into homes and over vehicles, 39,000 people were forced to **evacuate**. Although most were sad and scared to leave their homes, there are countless stories of neighbors helping each other, and sometimes strangers, too.

Hope in the Storm

Rescue missions happened every day during Hurricane Harvey. Federal forces rescued 10,000 people who were trapped in their homes or on flooded highways. At one point, the Houston Police Department's Dive Team rescued 3,000 people in four days. However, even the trained experts knew they needed help. Houston Police tweeted out to residents, "Anyone with a boat who can volunteer to help please call 712-881-3100" #HurricaneHarvey. People started up the boats in their driveways and began running their own rescue missions for members of their community. This also inspired the Cajun Navy to join—a group of volunteers from Louisiana arrived in Houston with 20 boats to help rescue people.

A group of Marines hands out supplies to a family outside of their flooded home in Orange, Texas.

Celebrity Hurricane Helpers

As the storm struck and the floodwaters rose, actors and musicians used their fame to raise money and awareness for the victims of Hurricane Harvey. Beyoncé, who was born in Houston, Texas, used her social media accounts to encourage people to give money to her fundraising campaign "BeyGood."

Houston Texans football player J.J. Watt posted several videos asking followers to donate to a "YouCaring" page, which other atheletes and celebrities supported. He ended up surpassing his goal of raising $200,000 and raised $37 million. He donated that money to AmeriCares, Feeding America, Save the Children, and SBP.

Houston-born Beyoncé encouraged fans to donate to hurricane relief.

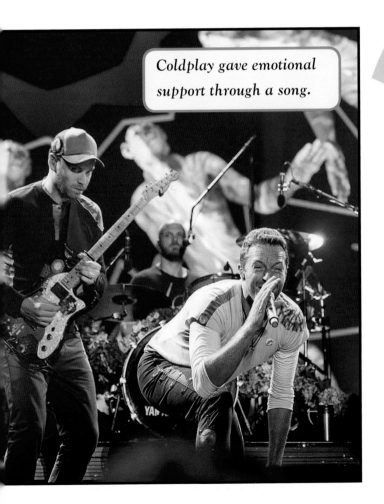

Coldplay gave emotional support through a song.

"The British rock band Coldplay had to cancel a show in Texas during the hurricane. As a tribute to the people there, they wrote a one-off country song called "Houston" and performed it live at their next concert. The lyrics were: "From Miami we are sending love to Houston; We are praying that you make it through the rain; I know nothing's gonna break the will of Houston; Oh, and we can't wait to go down there again."
– Lyrics in Coldplay song "Houston"

Escaping Danger

Drowning was only one risk during Hurricane Harvey. Drowning can happen in flooded homes, streets, or in cars while trying to escape. But there were other dangers that lurked in the floodwaters, as well.

Floating Disease-Makers

During floods such as those caused by Harvey, stormwaters overwhelm sanitary sewer systems, causing them to back up. **Bacteria** from human and animal waste can be carried in floodwaters. This creates health issues that could last long after the storm goes away. About 800 sewage treatment facilities were flooded during Harvey.

People waded through waste-strewn waters in the streets and in their homes. When tested, the **E. coli** levels in one flooded house were found to be 135 times what is considered safe. When objects are swept up by streaming floodwaters, people can be cut by sharp edges. This is extremely dangerous because bacteria in the water can cause **infections**.

Stranded in the Flood

One of the most shocking images of Harvey's destruction was of a group of elderly nursing home residents who were stranded in waist-deep floodwater in Dickinson, Texas. A plea for help was put out on Twitter. Emergency services then airlifted the residents and staff to safety. The elderly and handicapped are especially vulnerable during disasters. Many require special medical care, and they can't evacuate by themselves during emergencies.

The Louisiana National Guard helped local authorities to evacuate senior care homes across Texas.

Shelter from the Storm

Emergency shelters are designated safe places during disasters. There were 230 shelters open across Texas and Louisiana during the storm to help the 39, 000 people who needed a place to shelter. People slept there and received food while waiting for the storm and flood danger to pass. Some shelters were a haven of hope, while others began to develop their own safety concerns. Shelters are crowded places where people have no privacy. Some shelters had showers where people could wash. Most shelters were stocked with donations such as water and diapers.

Staying Positive

At the NRG Center in Houston, an emergency medical crew helped people deal with health issues. They supplied medication to those who did not have time to grab theirs before they evacuated. Sometimes, medical staff isolated patients who might spread flu viruses or infections. They even recruited a guitar player and bassist staying at the shelter to play some music and help keep the atmosphere cheerful. A calm environment helps everyone during a natural disaster while chaos is happening outside.

Some shelters remained open for weeks while people reorganized their lives.

The Aftermath

Even when the rain ended, Texas was not in the clear. For many people, the aftermath proved to be as devastating as evacuating had been. They returned to homes full of muck and wrecked furniture. The clean-up was difficult, expensive, and time-consuming.

Chaos After the Storm

Hurricane Harvey was not a "normal" hurricane. There was damage to 203,000 homes, and of that number, 12,700 were destroyed. The flooding also ruined a million vehicles. Many people still were not able to get back into their homes by mid September, because 3,900 homes still did not have power. As people were trying to move on with their lives, the community had some serious rebuilding to do. The impact was so big, that it would take a while for life to return to normal. There was flood damage to buildings that kept 75 out of 275 schools closed in Houston.

Many courtrooms were still closed for the same reason, backlogging the criminal justice system. Governments and organizations were also concerned about the long-term effect on people's health. There were dangerous molds that could start growing in moist conditions, pollution released from factories during the storm, and toxins in the floodwaters. No one knew what dangers from the hurricane lurked in the months and years ahead.

> *Flooded homes had to be thoroughly cleaned and dried out. In many cases, this meant stripping them down to their "bones."*

Stories of Loss

Loss was experienced in so many ways during Hurricane Harvey, including the loss of the sense of safety. At least 88 people in Texas lost their lives during the storm and in the unsafe conditions after the storm. Some people died while trying to save others. The heroic actions and kindness of others, and just knowing that others cared, helped ease the burden for some.

Stories of Hope

However, medical experts know that even when people experienced glimmers of hope during traumatic events such as Hurricane Harvey, there should still be concern for mental health after the storm. Medical experts prepared to talk to people in the weeks that followed, to help them manage the trauma they felt from enduring the storm. Some developed post traumatic stress disorder (PTSD), a mental health condition that can affect people after a scary or stressful event. People with PTSD can experience **flashbacks**, nightmares, anxiety, as well as physical conditions such as a racing heart.

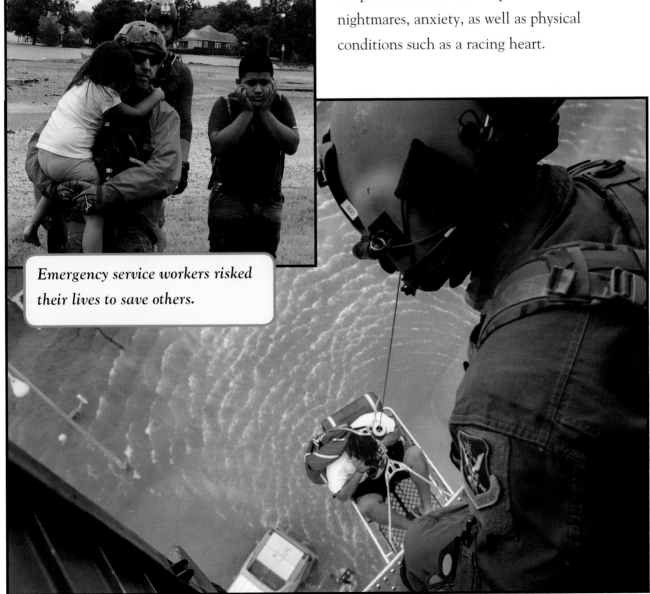

Emergency service workers risked their lives to save others.

Lessons from Harvey

Social media plays an increasingly important role in major events such as natural disasters. As Hurricane Harvey hit and hung over Texas for four days, social media became an important way for those affected to get information and to reach out for help.

Staying Social in the Storm

In many cases, it was also a way for people to take matters into their own hands. Citizens received updates from various organizations and agencies about the path of the storm and how to stay safe. People who needed help sent out tweets with the hashtags #sosHarvey and #helphouston so they could be found by citizen rescuers. People turned to Twitter when they were calling emergency numbers for help, but couldn't get through. Eventually, a Twitter account and a Google database were created, collecting the names and locations of people who needed help.

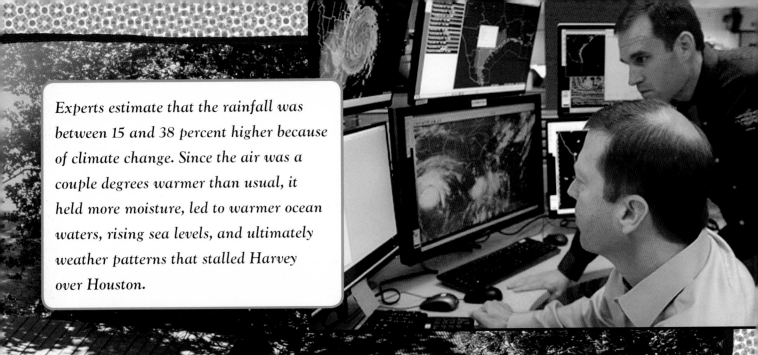

Experts estimate that the rainfall was between 15 and 38 percent higher because of climate change. Since the air was a couple degrees warmer than usual, it held more moisture, led to warmer ocean waters, rising sea levels, and ultimately weather patterns that stalled Harvey over Houston.

Safety Check

A new feature was added to Facebook in recent years called "Safety Check." In events such as natural disasters, this feature is activated by Facebook for people in the affected area. Facebook users can mark themselves as "safe" so their friends and family on Facebook can see that they are okay.

Flood Prevention

New discussions began at the political level to prevent the flooding during Hurricane Harvey from happening again. There were talks of new flood-control projects, such as building the "Ike Dike," a coastal barrier to protect Houston, Galveston, and the area's oil refineries and plants from **storm surges**, or abnormal rises of water during a storm. Another possibility is to build underground tunnels to help drain the floodwaters. However, when the summer of 2018 arrived, heavy rains and flooding once again became a problem for Houston residents.

Hurricane Irma

Before Hurricane Harvey had completely disappeared from satellite view, Hurricane Irma began forming in the Atlantic. It made its way through the Caribbean, starting off as a Category 2 hurricane, and quickly reaching a Category 5 – the most dangerous level.

Heartbreaking Loss

Irma's brutal destruction just didn't seem to end. It became the storm with the longest recorded history as a Category 5 hurricane. The storm raged through the Caribbean and nine southern states from August 31 to September 11. Irma's ferocity left a devastating number of deaths in the Caribbean and the United States. However, figuring out the exact number of deaths is a complicated process. People can be missing for days or months, making it difficult to make an official total. Also, experts need to determine whether each death was caused directly or indirectly by the hurricane.

After Hurricane Irma, it was determined that there was a total of 129 deaths, 44 of which, mostly in the Caribbean, were **directly** caused by the hurricane's winds. They reached speeds of up to 185 miles per hour (298 kph). The remaining 85 deaths, mostly in the United States, were **indirect** results of the hurricane, caused mostly by car crashes or electrocution.

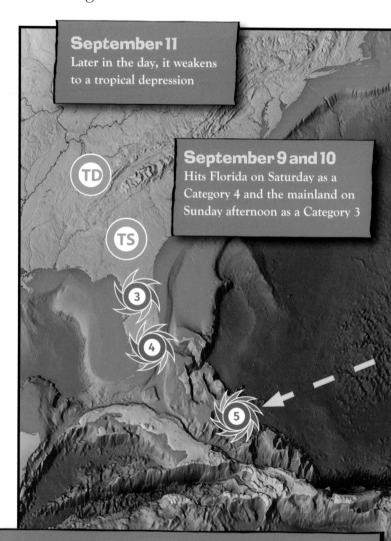

September 11
Later in the day, it weakens to a tropical depression

September 9 and 10
Hits Florida on Saturday as a Category 4 and the mainland on Sunday afternoon as a Category 3

Gaining Power

Hurricane Irma went through various stages as it developed into a Category 5 hurricane. Those stages, in terms of wind speed, are also referred to in the following ways:

Tropical depression: less than 39 miles per hour (63 kph)

Tropical storm: up to 73 miles per hour (117 kph)

Hurricane: up to 110 miles per hour (177 kph)

Major Hurricane: more than 110 miles per hour (177 kph)

Tracking Hurricane Irma

The development of Hurricane Irma had similar origins to that of Hurricane Harvey. It gained its strength from the warm waters of the Atlantic Ocean, and went on to spend 8.5 days as a major hurricane and 3.25 days as a Category 5 hurricane. This is the path along which Hurricane Irma transformed from a tropical wave to a major hurricane:

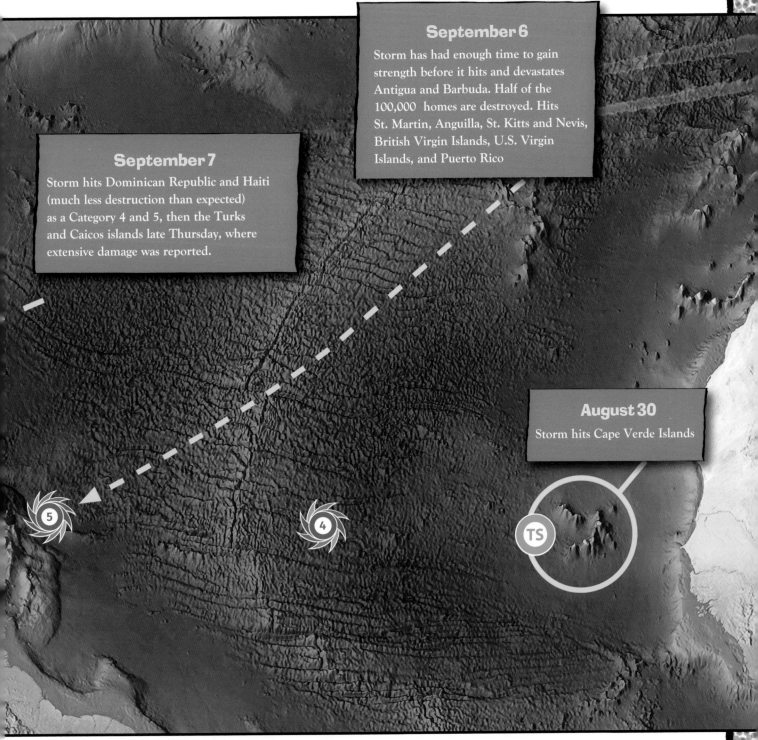

September 6

Storm has had enough time to gain strength before it hits and devastates Antigua and Barbuda. Half of the 100,000 homes are destroyed. Hits St. Martin, Anguilla, St. Kitts and Nevis, British Virgin Islands, U.S. Virgin Islands, and Puerto Rico

September 7

Storm hits Dominican Republic and Haiti (much less destruction than expected) as a Category 4 and 5, then the Turks and Caicos islands late Thursday, where extensive damage was reported.

August 30

Storm hits Cape Verde Islands

Irma in the Caribbean

Hurricane Irma was the strongest storm on record in the Atlantic. It caused catastrophic damage in the eastern Caribbean, affecting 1.2 million people and killing more than 30 people. By the time the storm had ripped through the area, the estimate for damages was as high as $3 billion.

Surviving Irma

Residents had prepared for the storm by stocking up on food and survival necessities and then sheltering themselves in their homes. Although the severity of damages differed from island to island, there were many places that suffered extensive power outages and looting due to food and water shortages. It was difficult for people to get service for their cell phones. People also feared the losses that would be suffered by the tourism industry—an important part of the Caribbean's economic stability.

In Cuba, many crops were destroyed, making people fear whether they would have enough food to feed their families. In Anguilla, 80 to 90 percent of the schools were damaged, meaning most would be closed for a long time. In Turks and Caicos islands, there was damage to the water treatment plant and hospitals. Drinking water and health care treatment was limited. In some places, there were even reports of prison breaks because of damage to prisons.

Barbuda Destruction

Barbuda is a small island in the eastern Caribbean that was hit particularly hard by Hurricane Irma. All 1,800 residents were evacuated to the island's southern neighbor, Antigua. This was an extraordinary event in itself because the people from each island have not always gotten along. But during Hurricane Irma, there were many stories of Antigua's residents welcoming their neighbors from Barbuda with kindness and hospitality. Two and a half months after the hurricane, Barbuda was still "uninhabitable" according to island leaders. It was estimated that 95 percent of properties were severely damaged, there was no electricity or water, and the animals that had survived the storm roamed freely around the island.

Wiping Out Land Ownership

There were calls from Barbuda's politicians for help from the rest of the world to rebuild their island. American actor Robert de Niro stepped up to gather support, but the government said the $5 million raised in immediate relief effort was not enough for the level of disaster Hurricane Irma left behind. To add to the tensions, as the evacuated people want to get back to their homes and rebuild, some were critical of the government's delay in returning people. Barbuda has long operated under a **shared-land model**, in which land is owned by all. Keen on **foreign investment**, the government wants to sell off land. Hurricanes such as Irma are sometimes just the start of irreparable change.

As small groups of people were allowed back to visit the island in October, they were devastated to find pets dead, houses destroyed, and beloved pictures gone.

Irma in Florida

Irma first hit Key West in Florida overnight from September 9 to September 10 as a Category 4 hurricane. It lost some strength as it moved inland. A state of emergency was declared on September 4 and many people evacuated. They quickly packed necessities, boarded up their homes, and hoped for the best as they left their properties in the path of Hurricane Irma.

Mass Evacuations

The evacuation order went out to 6.3 million people in Florida and the coast of Georgia as Hurricane Irma approached. Not everyone left, but some places such as Monroe County faced **mandatory** evacuation, where 31,000 people were forced to leave. An evacuation of that many people created problems across the state. Gas stations ran out of fuel and the traffic jams on roads and highways made it difficult to leave.

"If you're told to evacuate, leave, get out quickly... this storm is wider than our entire state... I cannot stress this enough – do not ignore evacuation orders. We can rebuild your home; we can't rebuild your life"
– Governor Rick Scott of Florida, on ABC News

People packed what they could in suitcases and bags, and headed out of town on any available transportation method.

Emergency service workers, including doctors, paramedics, and rescue workers, were transported by the Air Force.

Seeking Shelter

Floridians are experienced hurricane survivors. But many of those who had once felt confident staying in their own homes, changed their minds when a new forecast came out on the morning of September 9. Irma had picked up strength and was heading their way. Later that day, massive lineups had formed outside of more than 250 evacuation centers across the state. At one shelter in Germain Arena in Estero, thousands of evacuees waited in line outside to get a spot. The shelters were so overcrowded that evacuees had to travel to several different locations before they found one that still had space. This last-minute evacuation happened just in time. More than 6.8 million people lost power in their homes.

It's important to consider the needs of people who can't easily pick up and leave during a national disaster. Seniors, the disabled, and pets need shelters with special care.

Special Needs Shelters

One mother was relieved to find a shelter at a setup by the Department of Health, to accommodate individuals with special needs. Her son has cerebral palsy and uses feeding tubes for nutrition, and equipment to help him breathe. The gymnasium where they evacuated to provided generators so his medical equipment could work, clean bedding, a hygienic environment, and nurses to help with extra care.

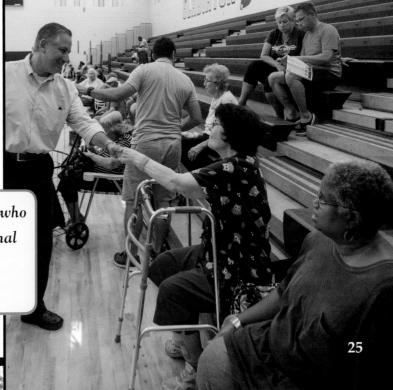

After Irma

The storm had passed, but the aftermath was worse than many had imagined, especially in the Florida Keys where Hurricane Irma had hit the hardest. Although evacuees were anxious to return to their homes, their communities were danger zones.

The Aftermath

There were hazards everywhere, from uprooted trees and fallen power lines, to remains of damaged buildings that could collapse. Returning home was a long process. Properties had to be assessed, delaying some people's return home for months. When they could go home, they found homes destroyed, or no running water and a sewage system that no longer functioned. There was still no electricity in many places, and as temperatures soared, a lack of air conditioning made things even more unbearable.

Those Left Behind

In the days following the hurricane, a tragic story came out of Hollywood, Florida, where 12 residents at a nursing home died of heat-related causes. The rehabilitation facility lost power and its air conditioner on September 10. By September 13, eight people had died, with four more to follow later that week. It prompted anger and questions over who was to blame for exposing elderly residents to the dangerous heat conditions. Following that, Governor Rick Scott signed a bill that required nursing homes to have backup power in case of power outages.

What Is FEMA?

FEMA, or the Federal Emergency Management Agency, is an agency of the United States Department of Homeland Security, which helps the federal government support state and local governments as they help citizens after a disaster.

Looking Back

When an evaluation of the storm happened in the weeks after Hurricane Irma, it was generally believed that the state of Florida did a good job evacuating people early, and opening and staffing evacuation centers. However, there was still much to question. Scientists wanted to know why the storm was as bad as it was and how it came so quickly after Hurricane Harvey.

After all, this was the first time in recorded American history that two major Category 4 hurricanes have hit in so short a time. Scientists wanted the world to pay attention to the possible effects of global warming. They warned that warming water temperatures and rising water levels are a factor in what is making hurricane season more dangerous to everyone in the path of hurricanes.

Five living former presidents, Bill Clinton, George W. Bush, George H.W. Bush (all pictured here), Jimmy Carter, and Barack Obama, came together to launch a fundraising campaign for hurricane relief. The campaign raised $42 million.

Hurricane Maria

Maria in the Caribbean

When Hurricane Maria ripped through the Caribbean, Puerto Rico and Dominica were still recovering from the devastation of Hurricane Irma. Maria hit Dominica as a Category 5 hurricane on September 18, then devastated Puerto Rico as a Category 4 hurricane on September 20.

Hurricane Maria hit the island of Dominica as a Category 5 hurricane. Most homes were damaged or destroyed.

Maria in Dominica

Hurricane Maria was the strongest hurricane on record to ever make landfall in Dominica, a Caribbean island in the West Indies. Maria intensified from a Category 1 to Category 5 storm in only two days. It arrived in Dominica on September 18, in the middle of the night. The storm's 160 mile per hour (257 kph) winds tore roofs off buildings. Torrential rainfall washed away soil, debris, and a bridge.

A small island with normally lush rainforests, Dominica lost a lot of trees and the Sisserou parrots that live there. In villages and the capital, building walls crumbled to the ground and roads heaved. About 95 percent of the buildings were damaged, including schools and hotel resorts that are part of the island's tourism industry. By early October, the death count was up to 27 people, but there were still 50 people missing.

Difficult Decisions

With so many buildings ruined, many employers shut down their businesses, leaving people without jobs. Some people decided to leave the island to start a new life elsewhere. For those who stayed, they faced power outages, food and water shortages, and being without a job. Mothers were fearful that they wouldn't be able to feed their children, since food was difficult to find.

Aid was greatly needed after Hurricane Maria brought ruin to Dominica. Money was pledged from the UK and U.N. agencies such as UNICEF. One very helpful supply was "school-in-a-box" kits for children, which included classroom materials in an aluminum case, such as a solar radio, inflatable globes, and blackboard lids.

Bringing Tourists Back

Dominica took many months to recover, including its tourism industry. People come from all over the world to see its volcano, waterfalls, and hot springs. With damage to buildings, roads, and trees, a lot of rebuilding was necessary to make it safe for visitors again. Buildings were rebuilt with stronger materials and animals such as the parrot started to return to the forests, but some roads were still difficult to travel on, and food **rations** were in place at many restaurants on the island for months after Maria.

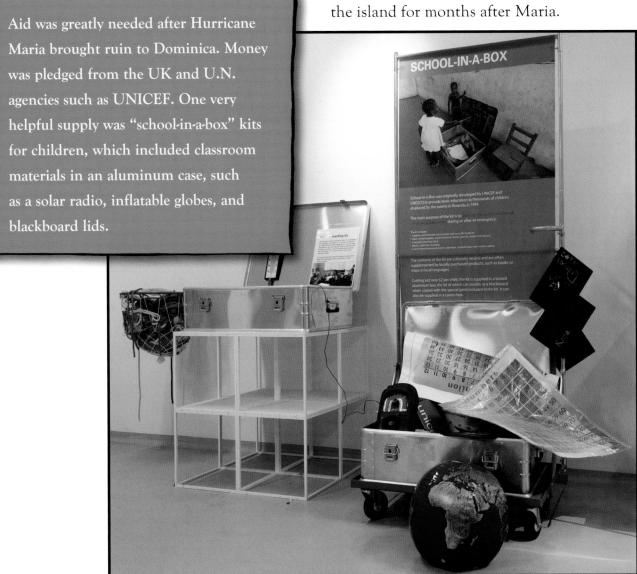

Devastation Again

The National Weather Service in the United States watched Hurricane Maria pummel Dominica as a Category 5 storm, and it began to warn people in Puerto Rico that they were right in its path. While they were still cleaning up from Irma, the people of Puerto Rico had to prepare for another assault.

Back to Disaster Mode

At least 60,000 people in Puerto Rico had to brace for Maria without power in their homes. They cleaned debris and rubble from the ground so it didn't become dangerous missiles when lifted by the strong winds of Maria. For many, there was no time to clean up. They scrambled to once again stock up on food and water.

The government of Puerto Rico opened 500 schools and other buildings to be used as shelters for at least 2,756 people to escape the path of Hurricane Maria. Washington sent 500 National Guard members to Puerto Rico for support, as well.

Hurricane Maria was an important reminder for many American citizens that Puerto Rico is a territory of the United States and Puerto Ricans are American citizens.

Maria was the strongest hurricane to hit Puerto Rico in more than 80 years, and the first Category 4 in 85 years.

Catastrophic Floods

Despite all the effort preparing, it wasn't enough to withstand the Category 4 that hit Puerto Rico at 6:15 a.m. on Wednesday, September 20. The maximum sustained winds were 155 miles per hour (249 kph) — so strong that they knocked out radar instruments on the ground. That meant meteorologists could only track the storm from satellites. From that view, meteorologists saw that the storm was the size of the entire island. Some parts of Puerto Rico saw 30 inches (76 cm) of rain in one day, which was the amount Houston received in three days during Hurricane Harvey.

The Aftermath

For months after Maria, the official death toll was set at 64. It wasn't until August 2018—almost a full year after the hurricane—that officials announced 2,975 had died. Some were killed directly from the storm. Many others died as a result of widespread power outages, supply shortages, and their inability to access the health care they needed. On an island that was devastated and barely coping, the lack of electricity and drinking water endangered lives.

Humanitarian Crisis

Puerto Rico's governor, Ricardo Rosselló spoke about the situation on the island, calling it a "humanitarian crisis." There were major food and water shortages after the storm, leaving 1.53 million people with no access to drinking water six days after the hurricane. In desperate searches for water, people drank dirty water. This lead to water-related disease outbreaks across the island.

The island's electrical system had been destroyed. Three million people were without power, some for months. There were some generators, but fuel was difficult to find. Many hospitals were damaged and closed. Only 15 percent of the island's 69 hospitals were open, leaving people without health care.

> " The San Juan that we knew yesterday is no longer here.
> – Mayor Carmen Yulin Cruz told MSNBC, referring to Puerto Rico's capital and largest city. "

A Dire Situation

A Category 4 hurricane would be devastating for any region, but what made Hurricane Maria even worse in Puerto Rico was that the island was already struggling with an economic crisis before Irma and Maria hit. The government of Puerto Rico could not pay its debts. Additional costs from the storm reached into the billions, and the island's main industries of agriculture and tourism were badly damaged by the storm. Crops were ruined, hotels were damaged, and like the rest of the island, without electricity. The island's communication system was knocked out, which meant phones, Internet, and banking systems were down. Even if an ambulance could have made it through the streets to an open hospital, people had no way to call the ambulance.

Help and Hope Needed

Help did come. Puerto Rico received $5 billion from the federal government to help with relief efforts. Three days after Hurricane Maria, 11 ships arrived with "1.6 million gallons (6 million liters) of water, 23,000 cots, [and] dozens of generators" according to the Associated Press. President Donald Trump visited the island five days after the hurricane. Some people question whether FEMA and the government did enough for Puerto Rico. Although money and resources were sent, people were left without running water and power for months, and it became the longest major power outage in U.S. history.

In the aftermath of the hurricanes, Puerto Rican celebrities began using their platforms to draw the world's attention to Puerto Rico. One example of this was Lin-Manuel Miranda, an American composer with Puerto Rican ancestry, who composed a song called "Almost Like Praying." Two things made this song extra special: first, the melody was sung by 22 famous Latino artists including Jennifer Lopez, Camila Cabello, Gloria Estefan, and Marc Anthony. Second, the money made from the song was donated to the Hispanic Federation which provided relief efforts to Puerto Rico after Hurricane Maria.

Camila Cabello sang on a recording that raised funds for hurricane relief.

A Terrible Toll

Puerto Rico has suffered terribly since Irma and Maria. Many people have been **displaced**, or forced from their homes. But Puerto Ricans have also proven amazingly **resilient**, living in very difficult conditions but still banding together to provide support to each other.

Dam Burst

With its infrastructure in tatters, Puerto Rico was faced with another challenge: evacuating 70,000 people living near the Guajataca Dam before it crumbled and burst. The evacuation order came after engineers spotted cracks in the 88-year-old structure. As water levels had increased in height after Hurricane Maria, the reservoir behind the dam was swelling. Eventually, the dam gave way to massive gushes of water.

Death Toll Disputed

After the storm passed, the official death toll was said to be 64. That number was revised to 2,975 in August 2018 after Puerto Rico's governor hired researchers from George Washington University to produce an accurate estimate of the death toll. One of the goals of the report was to highlight services that could be strengthened before future hurricanes. A Harvard University study published in the *New England Journal of Medicine* in July 2018 estimated the death count could be as high as 4, 645. That study counted indirect deaths, and included people who had health conditions such as kidney disease that had been made worse after the hurricane because of lack of proper health care, electricity, and medicines.

The Guajataca Dam before cracks led to it crumbling and flooding.

Chronic Disaster Syndrome

Where does Puerto Rico go from there? A more accurate death toll helps researchers learn more about risk factors during and after hurricanes. That can assist with the way families, communities, and governments prepare for, and survive after, hurricanes. A study published in 2009 revealed that many people who had to endure long-term damage for years after Hurricane Katrina, followed by Hurricane Rita, suffer from what has been called "chronic disaster syndrome." This condition can appear in individuals who have suffered near-death events, loss of loved ones, loss of homes and jobs, and economic instability. In short, "disaster mode" is the only way in which people know how to live, and it's extremely stressful on their bodies and minds. As the future of Puerto Rico appears to have a long-term road to recovery, in factors ranging from loss of life, to loss of structures to economic failure, "chronic disaster syndrome" may be a greater public health concern.

Leaving the Island

With an overwhelming sense of hopelessness among communities, many people left Puerto Rico for jobs and safety in the mainland United States. Their loss makes the rebuilding process more difficult. In a PBS interview after the 2017 hurricanes, one person talked about their community feeling empty because so many people were leaving. They saw no future there for themselves or their families. For those who remained, many were still sleeping on their balconies, in their cars or in shelters, because their homes were uninhabitable.

Hurricane Nate

Hurricane Nate was the ninth hurricane of the 2017 season when it made landfall in the United States on Saturday, September 7, as a Category 1 storm. It was also the first time a hurricane made landfall in Mississippi since Hurricane Katrina in 2005. Hurricane Nate developed in the southern Caribbean and moved north toward the Gulf of Mexico, passing through Central America on Thursday, October 5.

Central America Hit

Central America suffered tragically when 44 people were killed in Costa Rica, Nicaragua, Panama, Guatemala, El Salvador, and Honduras. Hurricane Nate was particularly devastating, although when it passed through these countries it was only a "tropical storm." It was the damages that followed the storm that were particularly devastating—heavy rains, flooding, landslides, and mudslides, as well as destroyed bridges and damaged houses.

The clean-up from a hurricane such as Nate can take months.

Crocodiles resting in the overflow of the Tarcoles River.

What Is a Mudslide?

Hundreds of people had to be saved from **mudslides** after the storm's first pass. A mudslide occurs when wet earth suddenly moves down the side of a mountain or hill. Mudslides are another form of natural disaster that can be powerful and deadly, because they can cause mass destruction in a short time. Mudslides happen often in the United States. There is even a mudslide season in California. Mudslides are common during heavy rains or structural changes to a slope that rain runs down, such as after the damage of Nate. A **landslide**, by contrast, can occur in dry or wet conditions. It is the massive movement of earth, rock, and soil down the side of a mountain or hill.

Facing Hardships

Hurricane Nate was yet another reminder of the different impacts that natural disasters can have on different countries and communities. Life after Nate for countries in Central America brought new hardships after the original chaos of the storm passed. Schools were closed across all of Nicaragua.

In Costa Rica, 5,000 people sought shelter and 400,000 people were left without clean water. There were also concerns over crocodiles making their way inland as the Tarcoles River in Costa Rica had overflowed, bringing unknown items and creatures with it.

Nate in the U.S.

Some warned that Nate could undergo rapid intensification if it moved slowly over the warm waters of the ocean on its way to the United States. At that point in the season, hurricanes Harvey, Irma, and Maria had all rapidly intensified and posed much greater threats. Nate's storm system changed course suddenly after leaving Central America and it headed directly for New Orleans, where Hurricane Katrina had hit in 2005.

Not Taking Chances

After a season of hurricane devastation across the U.S., nobody wanted to take chances with Nate. Tropical storm warnings were given to the coastlines of Louisiana, Mississippi, and Alabama. Even Florida prepared for the storm, although they were no longer in the predicted path. The preparations took the form of evacuation orders for people who lived in New Orleans, outside the city's storm protection system, which is a series of floodgates in low-lying areas. The National Guard mobilized 1,300 troops and prepared boats and school buses that could operate in high water to rescue people stranded during flooding or storm surges. Mandatory curfews on the Gulf Coast of Alabama kept people safe while the storm moved closer. Airports were also closed in Florida and Alabama.

Nate was the fastest-moving tropical storm in the Gulf of Mexico. It followed a northwesterly path at 29 miles per hour (47 kph) from the western Caribbean through Central America and the Gulf Coast, before heading northeast and losing strength.

Closing Oil Refineries

Before the hurricane hit, there were preparations being made at oil refineries along the Gulf Coast. To evacuate workers to safety, 44 percent of oil and gas platforms in the Gulf of Mexico were shut down. This number of closed refineries grew as the storm grew closer and fears of the destruction it would cause increased. Although no serious damage was done, 92 percent of oil refineries were shut down and evacuated.

The storm surge from Hurricane Katrina in 2005 killed many people in their homes in New Orleans. Emergency responders feared Nate would cause almost as much harm.

Storm Surges

One fear during the preparation was the possibility of storm surges. FEMA warned that the many hurricanes of the season meant 85 percent of their resources were being used. This was concerning when there were predictions of 10-foot (3 m) storm surges in places such as Venetian Isles, which is a low-lying neighborhood in New Orleans.

The National Hurricane Center says storm surges can be the greatest threat to life and property during a hurricane. Storm surges killed 1,500 people during Hurricane Katrina in 2005. Storm surges can rise well above the height of average tides and causes extreme flooding in communities near a coastline.

Nate Makes Landfall

Hurricane Nate first hit late at night on Saturday, October 7, at the mouth of the Mississippi River. While 1,100 people in Mississippi were spending the night in shelters, the National Hurricane Center said Nate was expected to make another landfall.

Power's Out

Across Mississippi, 3,500 power outages happened before Hurricane Nate made its second landfall outside Biloxi, Mississippi. Winds ripped at 85 mph (137 kph). It soon weakened to a tropical depression, but 17,000 people in Mississippi did not have power. Not long after, the storm surges began. Along the coast of Mississippi and Alabama, some places experienced 6 to 9 feet (1.8–2.7 m) of flooding due to storm surges.

Better Than Expected?

Close to 60,000 homes and businesses across Mississippi, Alabama, Florida, and Georgia didn't have power by Sunday evening. While two deaths were indirectly connected to the storm due to traffic accidents, there were no casualties directly linked to the storm. Many places in the U.S. speak of Hurricane Nate as "dodging a bullet." Of the 48 deaths overall, two were attributed to the storm in the U.S., and 14 people died in Costa Rica.

Nate caused an estimated $2.5 billion in damages, wrecking roads and flooding homes and businesses.

Learning from History

Damages in Mississippi would have been much worse if extra safety measures hadn't been put in place after the devastation of Hurricane Katrina. Nearly $14 billion was invested in a federal hurricane protection system. Buildings were built higher off the ground, as well. In preparation for Hurricane Nate, officials knew better how to work together to prevent loss of structures and life. Emergency staff and first responders were prepared and waiting to jump into action. The hurricane protection system also meant skilled workers were ready to fix electrical grids if damaged. Medical staff were on hand to aid in injuries, and sewer workers were on standby to deal with flooding. A full force of hurricane preparedness staff worked around the clock to fix the drainage pumps to help with flooding.

Katrina's Legacy

When Hurricane Katrina struck the Gulf Coast in August 2005, it affected the lives of hundreds of thousands of people in Louisiana, Mississippi, and Alabama for more than 10 years. A devastating Category 3 hurricane when it hit, Katrina was directly and indirectly responsible for 1,833 deaths. It caused more than $100 billion in damage. The aftermath of the storm was especially destructive. In New Orleans, 80 percent of the city flooded after levees failed. Along the Gulf Coast, recovery efforts lasted more than 10 years. The government and FEMA received much criticism about its slow response to help citizens in New Orleans as a disaster zone unfolded. Many lessons were learned from Hurricane Katrina and its aftermath. It affected the way preparations and recovery for Hurricane Nate were handled.

Louisiana National Guard make preparations for Hurricane Nate.

A Safe Future For All

Each major hurricane of 2017 showed how different communities react and adjust to disaster. The more prepared a place is, and the more resources it has—financially and in human power—the better the outcomes.

Some People Hurt More

It's a documented fact that some groups of people suffer more during natural disasters. These groups include ethnic minorities, people with language barriers, individuals with disabilities, pregnant women, children, the elderly, and the poor.

Law professor and **bioethicist** Sharona Hoffman has studied disaster readiness and says people in these groups need to be included in disaster planning. Many of those who died during Hurricane Katrina were unable to evacuate because they could not walk and had no one to help them. Some didn't want to leave pets or possessions behind.

Hoffman says ensuring shelters and temporary housing are suitable for people with handicaps, and providing accessible evacuation transportation, should be a part of disaster planning. Inequality can become more emphasized during natural disasters. Vulnerable groups often have less access to resources that could help them overcome suffering, such as money and support networks, and often aren't aware of the services available to them.

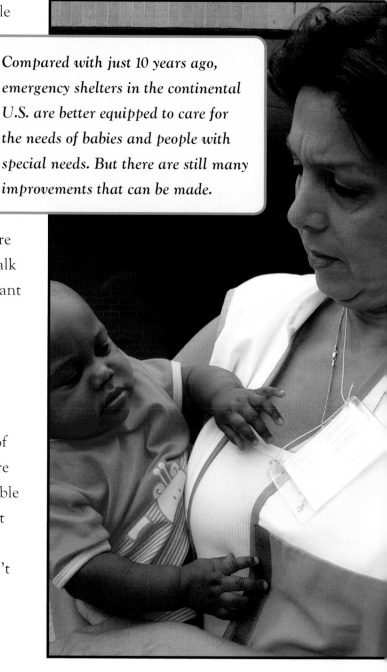

Compared with just 10 years ago, emergency shelters in the continental U.S. are better equipped to care for the needs of babies and people with special needs. But there are still many improvements that can be made.

Hurricanes and Climate Change

After each major hurricane during the 2017 hurricane season, scientists and meteorologists emphasized how warming oceans are intensifying tropical storms, and perhaps making them more frequent.

While scientists are not claiming that hurricanes are a direct result of climate change, many argue that increased wind speeds, higher storm surges, and increased rainfall are factors to look out for in the future as climate change continues to affect the environment.

Do You Want to Make a Difference?

To protect our fellow humans and our Earth from the destruction of more major hurricanes in the future, there are some things you can do to help stop the progress of climate change. According to the David Suzuki Foundation:

1. Talk to your local politicians about how important climate change is to you.
2. Remember to turn off the lights when you leave a room or unplug your electronic devices when not in use.
3. Learn more about renewable energy such as wind farms or solar power.
4. Choose organic and locally grown foods.
5. Produce less waste to keep landfills at lower levels of trash.
6. Walk, ride a bike, or take public transportation instead of a car, if you can.

Hurricane Prepping

For those living in areas that experience hurricane season, there are steps that you and your family can take to prepare for a hurricane if it strikes. Both FEMA and the Red Cross suggest building a family emergency kit.

Build a Kit

To begin your family's kit, find a water-proof air-tight plastic bag, or a large plastic container to store all your materials. Next, fill it with the following essentials:

- Water: 1 gallon (3.8 liters) of water per person per day for at least three days, for drinking and sanitation
- Food: at least a three-day supply of non-perishable food
- Battery-powered or hand-crank radio, and a NOAA Weather Radio with tone alert
- Flashlight
- First aid kit
- Extra batteries
- Whistle to signal for help
- Dust mask to help filter contaminated air, and plastic sheeting and duct tape to shelter in-place
- Moist towelettes, garbage bags, and plastic ties for personal sanitation
- Wrench or pliers to turn off utilities
- Manual can opener for food
- Local maps

Staying Safe After a Hurricane:

Throughout this book, many examples were given of hurricane aftermaths that were just as dangerous as, if not more dangerous than, the storm itself. It can be shocking when people see their surroundings after a hurricane. There may be flooding, vehicles tossed around, bare trees where leaves were stripped, houses destroyed, possessions lost, and worst of all, lives taken. Even after the storm has passed, it does not mean dangers don't linger. The Red Cross also prepares people to stay safe after a hurricane with the following steps:

- Let your friends and family know you're safe. Register yourself as "safe" on Facebook's "Safety Check."
- If evacuated, return only when authorities say it is safe to do so.
- Continue listening to local news or a NOAA Weather Radio for updated information and instructions.
- Stay alert for extended rainfall and subsequent flooding.

Glossary

Note: Some boldfaced words are defined where they appear in the text.

air pressure The force exerted on a surface by the weight of the air

atmosphere The layers of gases that surround Earth

bacteria Microscopic living things, some of which can cause disease

basin A circular dip that is smaller at the bottom and larger at the top

bioethicist A scientist who studies the moral principles of medical and biological research

circulating Moving around

coordinates A group of numbers used to indicate the position of something on a map

dams Barriers that obstruct or confine the flow of water

E. coli A type of bacteria found in human and animal waste

evacuate To leave a place because of danger or disaster

flashbacks Recurring vivid memories of something, especially a traumatic experience

foreign investment Money from foreign countries used to make more money

infections Contamination with disease

mandatory Required, often by law, threats, or force

meteorologist Someone who uses data and scientific equipment to predict the weather

precipitation Falling condensation such as rain

rapid intensification Quickly growing in strength

rations A fixed amount of food given out during times of shortage and emergency

reservoirs Places where water is stored

resilient Able to withstand and recover quickly from difficult conditions

shared-land model A form of land ownership in which the land is owned equally by all, or shared equally

slow-moving storm Tropical storms or hurricanes that move slowly near a coast or inland and that usually drop more rain over a longer period of time

suburb An outlying part of a city, where many people live

tropical Wet and humid, close to the equator

tropical depression A low-pressure system in the tropics north and south of the equator

tropical wave An area or trough of low air pressure which moves east to west across the tropics and creates thunderstorms and cyclones

World Meteorological Organization An organization that studies worldwide weather and climate

wreak havoc To cause great damage

Learning More

BOOKS

Furgang, Kathy. *National Geographic Kids: Everything Weather.* National Geographic Kids, 2012.

Kostigen, Thomas M. *Extreme Weather: Surviving Tornadoes, Sandstorms, Blizzards, Hurricanes, and More!* National Geographic Kids, 2014.

Peppas, Lynn. *Disaster Alert! Superstorm Sandy.* Crabtree Publishing, 2014.

WEBSITES

https::/ /oceanservice.noaa.gov/hazards/sandy/
The National Oceanic and Atmospheric Administration (NOAA) is a U.S. government weather science agency. Their website offers photos, maps, videos, and updates on the effects of Superstorm Sandy.

www.enchantedlearning.com/subjects/weather/hurricane/
This Enchanted Learning website gives readers a full explanation of the science of hurricanes.

www.fema.gov
FEMA's website has a checklist of steps to take to prepare for a possible hurricane.

Index